The Car Boot Sale

Written by Narinder Dhami

Illustrated by Parwinder Singh

Collins

"We need some extra cash for our camping trip, Amba," Mum sighed.

"Let's find stuff to sell at the car boot sale."

Amba made a big pile of books, games, toys and jigsaws.

She put aside the items she
wanted to keep.

"Stripe can go," Amba said. "I'm too old for a toy tiger!"

The next day they woke up at dawn.
Amba could not stop yawning.

It was a fine June day as Mum drove to the car boot sale.

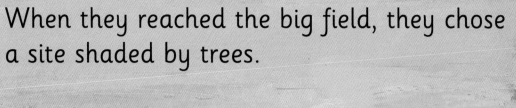

When they reached the big field, they chose a site shaded by trees.

They displayed the items they had for sale.

"Hello, how much is the tiger?" a customer said.

"Five pounds," Amba replied.

But then Amba felt dismayed. She had made a mistake. She did not want to sell Stripe!

The customer left without Stripe.
Amba sighed with relief. She could take
Stripe home!

But the customer's little dog had escaped his lead. He swiped Stripe and ran off.

"That dog stole Stripe!" Amba shrieked.
"Stop, thief!" She chased him.

The dog was chewing Stripe's paw.
Amba saw the little boy reach out
and save Stripe.

"Bad dog, Duke!" the boy's mum scolded.

"Hello, what's your name?" asked Amba.
"This is Stripe."

The little boy remained silent.

"Leo's not being rude," his mum explained.
"He has a few problems with speaking."

"Stripe," Leo muttered.

"Stripe likes you, Leo," said Amba. "He says you are his new keeper."

Leo and Amba both smiled.

Amba and Stripe

🐾 Review: After reading 🐾

Use your assessment from hearing the children read to choose any GPCs, words or tricky words that need additional practice.

Read 1: Decoding

- Turn to page 12 and point to the word **dismayed** Ask: Can you work out what Amba was feeling? What other word with a similar meaning could we use instead?
    - Encourage the children to reread the page for context.
    - Ask the children to offer synonyms (words with a similar meaning). (*horrified, upset, shocked*)
    - Encourage the children to try out their ideas by rereading the sentence with their own word in place of **dismayed**. Ask: Does it still make sense?
- Ask the children to sound out and read these words. Ask: Which word contains the /yoo/ sound? (**Duke**)
    mistake   thief   rude   Duke   silent   shaded
- Point to words with long vowel sounds at random, and ask: Can you blend in your head when you read this word?

Read 2: Prosody

- Challenge the children to read pages 14 and 15 dramatically, as if they were a storyteller on the radio, and need to hold the listener's attention.
- Model using expression for the sudden and surprise event on page 14. Ask the children to read after you.
- Model a different voice for Amba on page 15. Point to the word **shrieked**. Ask the children to read page 15 with expression and drama.

Read 3: Comprehension

- Return to the title of the story and let the children describe any car boot or other second-hand sales events they have seen. Ask: What might you sell at a sale?
- Reread pages 20 and 21, then encourage the children to talk about how Amba is kind. Ask the children to describe their own experiences of being kind, or people being kind to them.
- Say: Look back at the story and tell me if these statements are untrue. If untrue, what might be the true answer?
    - Amba didn't want the customer to buy Stripe because she could get more money selling it to someone else. (*untrue, e.g. she realised she didn't want to part with Stripe*)
    - Amba changed her mind and let Leo keep Stripe. (*true*)
- Turn to pages 22 and 23. Ask the children to use the pictures to help them retell the story in their own words.